Airplanes

by Thomas K. Adamson

BELLWETHER MEDIA • MINNEAPOLIS, MN

Note to Librarians, Teachers, and Parents:

Blastoff! Readers are carefully developed by literacy experts and combine standards-based content with developmentally appropriate text.

Level 1 provides the most support through repetition of high-frequency words, light text, predictable sentence patterns, and strong visual support.

Level 2 offers early readers a bit more challenge through varied simple sentences, increased text load, and less repetition of high-frequency words.

Level 3 advances early-fluent readers toward fluency through increased text and concept load, less reliance on visuals, longer sentences, and more literary language.

Level 4 builds reading stamina by providing more text per page, increased use of punctuation, greater variation in sentence patterns, and increasingly challenging vocabulary.

Level 5 encourages children to move from "learning to read" to "reading to learn" by providing even more text, varied writing styles, and less familiar topics.

Whichever book is right for your reader, Blastoff! Readers are the perfect books to build confidence and encourage a love of reading that will last a lifetime!

This edition first published in 2017 by Bellwether Media, Inc.

No part of this publication may be reproduced in whole or in part without written permission of the publisher. For information regarding permission, write to Bellwether Media, Inc., Attention: Permissions Department, 5357 Penn Avenue South, Minneapolis, MN 55419.

Library of Congress Cataloging-in-Publication Data

Names: Adamson, Thomas K., 1970- author.
Title: Airplanes / by Thomas K. Adamson.
Description: Minneapolis, MN : Bellwether Media, Inc., 2017. | Series: Blastoff! Readers: Mighty Machines in Action | Audience: Ages 5-8. | Audience: K to grade 3. | Includes bibliographical references and index.
Identifiers: LCCN 2016033330 (print) | LCCN 2016034283 (ebook) | ISBN 9781626175990 (hardcover : alk. paper) | ISBN 9781681033297 (ebook)
Subjects: LCSH: Airplanes–Juvenile literature.
Classification: LCC TL547 .A37 2017 (print) | LCC TL547 (ebook) | DDC 629.133/34–dc23
LC record available at https://lccn.loc.gov/2016033330

Editor: Christina Leighton   Designer: Steve Porter

Printed in the United States of America, North Mankato, MN.

Table of Contents

TAKEOFF!

An airplane speeds along the **runway**. Wings help the plane lift into the air.

wing

It soars more than 30,000 feet (9,144 meters) above the ground. What a view!

Soon, the airplane gets
ready to land. Its wheels
come out.

wheels

runway

The plane lands with a bump
and slows down on the long
runway. It has arrived!

AIRPLANES IN ACTION

Airplanes fly in the air over land and water. They carry people and **cargo**.

Some fly across the world.
Others take shorter trips.

THE LARGEST CARGO PLANE

Antonov AN-225 Mriya

length: 275.6 feet (84 meters)

average school bus

wingspan: 290 feet (88.4 meters)

Planes come in different
sizes. Big passenger
planes carry many people.

MACHINE PROFILE
BOEING 747-400

length: 231.8 feet (70.6 meters)
height: 63.7 feet (19.4 meters)
total passengers: up to 660
top speed: 614 miles (988 kilometers) per hour

Small planes fly to places that are hard to reach.

Airplanes may deliver mail or take **aerial** photographs. Some put out forest fires.

fighter jets

Airplanes also help the military.
Fighter jets battle enemies.

WINGS, WHEELS, AND ENGINES

An airplane has a tail and wings with **flaps**.

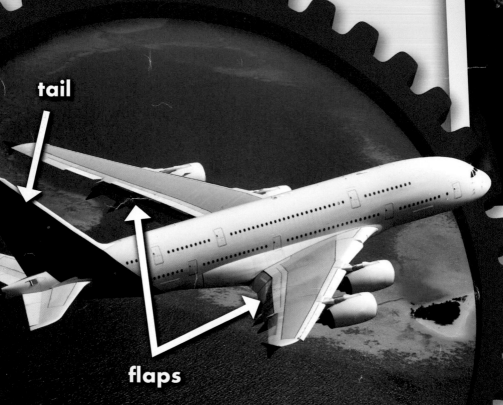

tail

flaps

cockpit

Pilots control these parts to fly the plane. They sit in the plane's **cockpit**.

Most planes have wheels for landing. They screech on the runway.

wheels

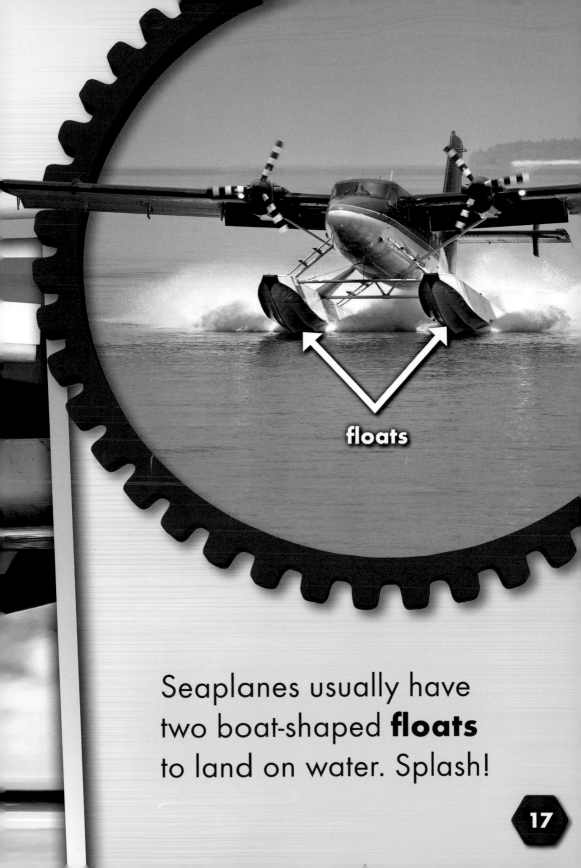

floats

Seaplanes usually have two boat-shaped **floats** to land on water. Splash!

propeller

Engines push air backward to move planes forward. Some planes have engines with **propellers**.

Others have **jet engines**. These are louder and more powerful.

IDENTIFY AN AIRPLANE

cockpit

tail

wing

jet engine

Airplanes have many jobs.
They buzz close to the ground
or zoom high across the sky.

These machines soar to great heights!

Glossary

aerial—from the air

cargo—something that is carried by an airplane

cockpit—the part of the airplane where the pilot sits

fighter jets—military airplanes used in battle

flaps—pieces of material on the wings of an airplane

floats—the boat-shaped parts under a seaplane that help it float on water

jet engines—engines that are powered by a stream of hot gases and air

pilots—people who fly airplanes

propellers—sets of spinning blades

runway—a long strip of pavement that airplanes use to take off and land

To Learn More

AT THE LIBRARY

Brown, Jordan D. *How Airplanes Get from Here... to There!* New York, N.Y.: Simon Spotlight, 2016.

McBriarty, Patrick T., and Johanna H. Kim. *Airplanes Take Off and Land.* Mansfield, Mass.: CurlyQ Press, 2015.

Salzmann, Mary Elizabeth. *Aircraft.* Minneapolis, Minn.: Sandcastle, 2016.

ON THE WEB

Learning more about airplanes is as easy as 1, 2, 3.

1. Go to www.factsurfer.com.

2. Enter "airplanes" into the search box.

3. Click the "Surf" button and you will see a list of related web sites.

With factsurfer.com, finding more information is just a click away.

Index